COMPUTERS

OUR LIFELINE

B

MANOJ PUBLICATIONS

COMPUTERS
Our Lifeline - B

Publisher :
MANOJ PUBLICATIONS

761, Main Road, Burari, Delhi-110084
Ph.   : 27611116, 27611349
Fax   : 27611546, Mob. : 9868112194
email   : info@manojpublications.com
Website : www.manojpublications.com

Showroom :

1583-84, Dariba Kalan, Chandni Chowk, Delhi-110006
Ph. : 23262174, 23268216
Mobile : 9818753569

ISBN 978-81-310-1951-1

Concept:
Puneet Gupta
M.B.A. (William & Mary, U.S.A.)

Edited by:
Davinder Singh Minhas

PREFACE

Learning computers is a must in today's Machine Age. Each and every work is being done with the use of different machines in the form of computers, LEDs, washing machines, microwave ovens, electric tandoor, mobile phones and so on. The list is endless and each new day dawns with a new invention, another new machine. So, it becomes imperative for every child to be familiar with the working knowledge of computers. There is no denying the fact that a little knowledge of computers makes our work easier and faster.

In this fast-paced life where computers have made their presence felt in every nook and corner of the world, a child's sound knowledge of computers stands him in good stead in the long run.

The present book is meant for the tiny tots who have just entered into the world of learning. Apart from the knowledge of other subjects, their familiarity with the concepts of computers at their tender age goes a long way in making them computer literates.

The book has been designed beautifully, keeping in mind the age-group at every stage of the book. We are more than sure that the book will come up to the expectations of the teacher and the taught. We shall be very much glad to entertain any constructive suggestion.

–Publisher

Contents

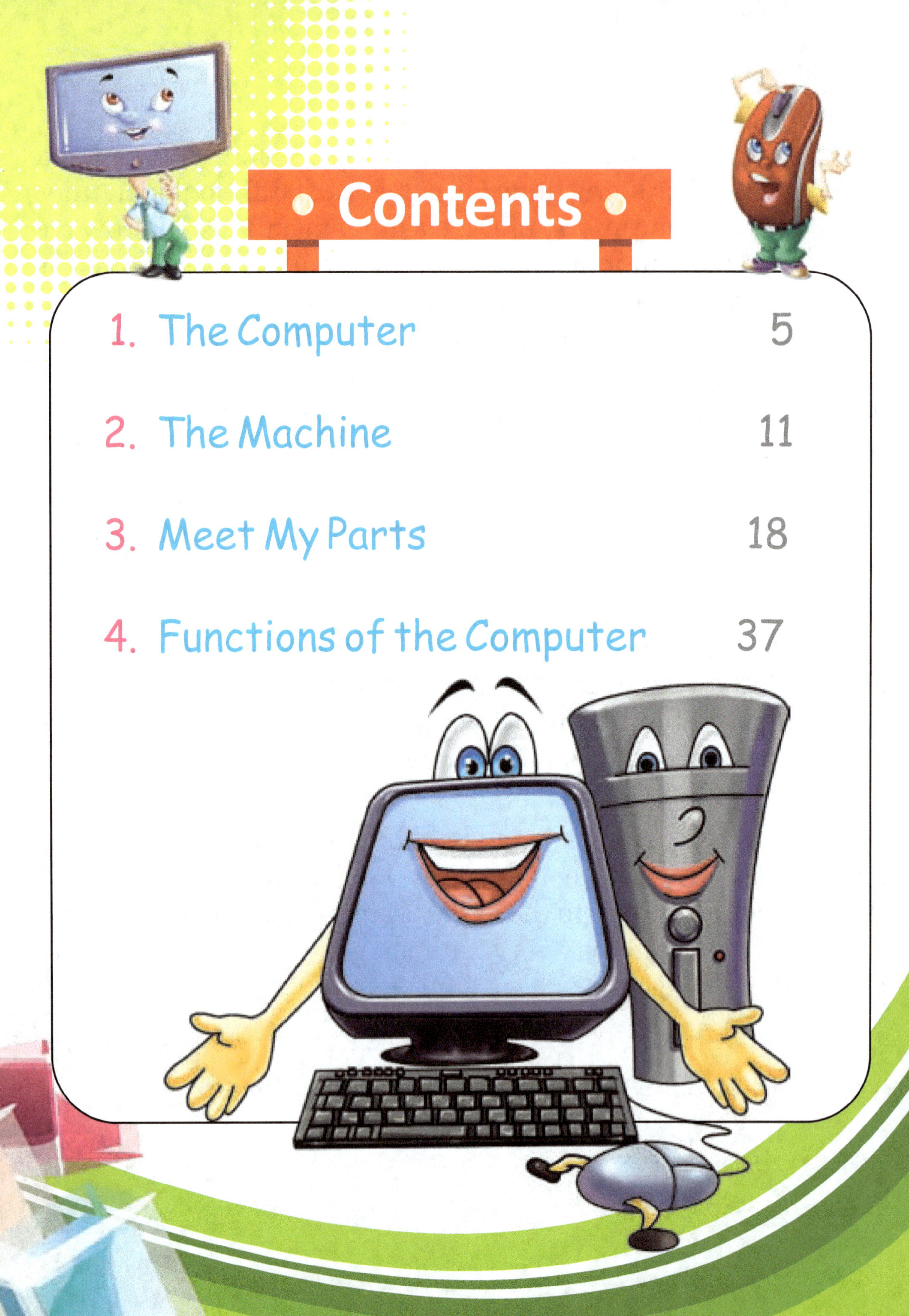

1. The Computer — 5

2. The Machine — 11

3. Meet My Parts — 18

4. Functions of the Computer — 37

THE COMPUTER

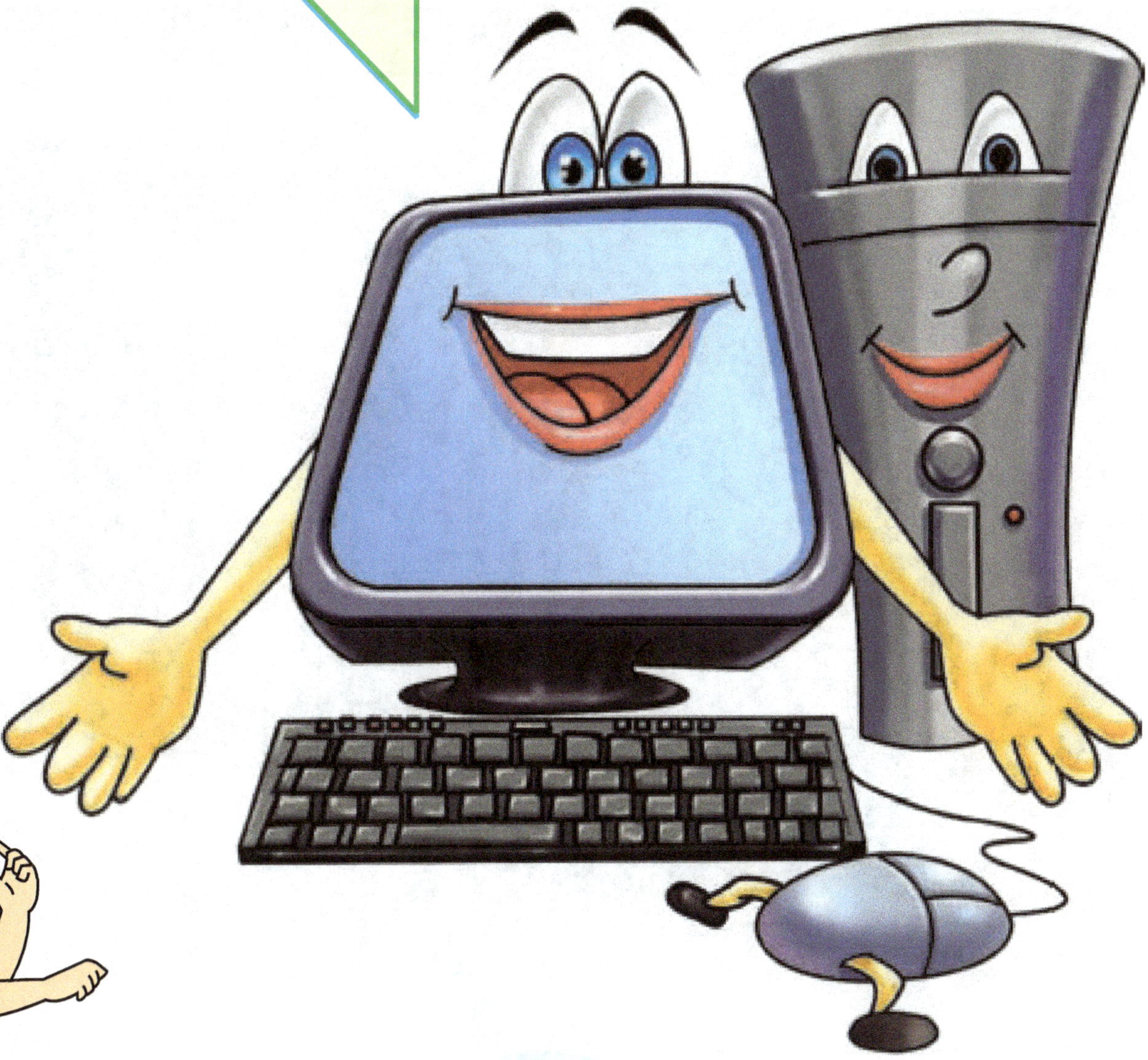

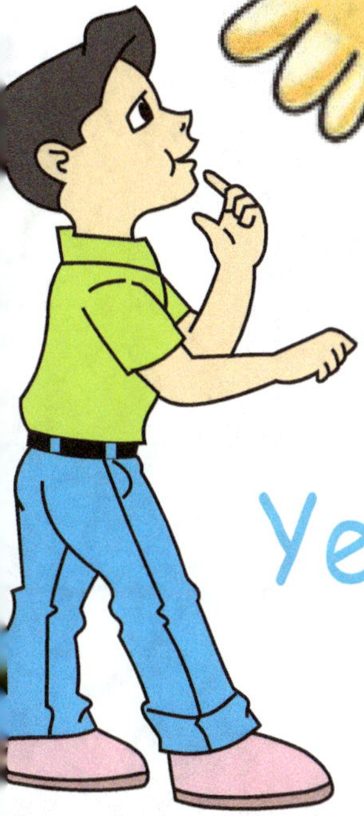

Yes, you are absolutely correct.

I am a **Computer**.

My name is Compy.
I am your friend. 
I shall teach you
to learn about me.

Join the numbers 1 to 12 and see what comes in front of you.

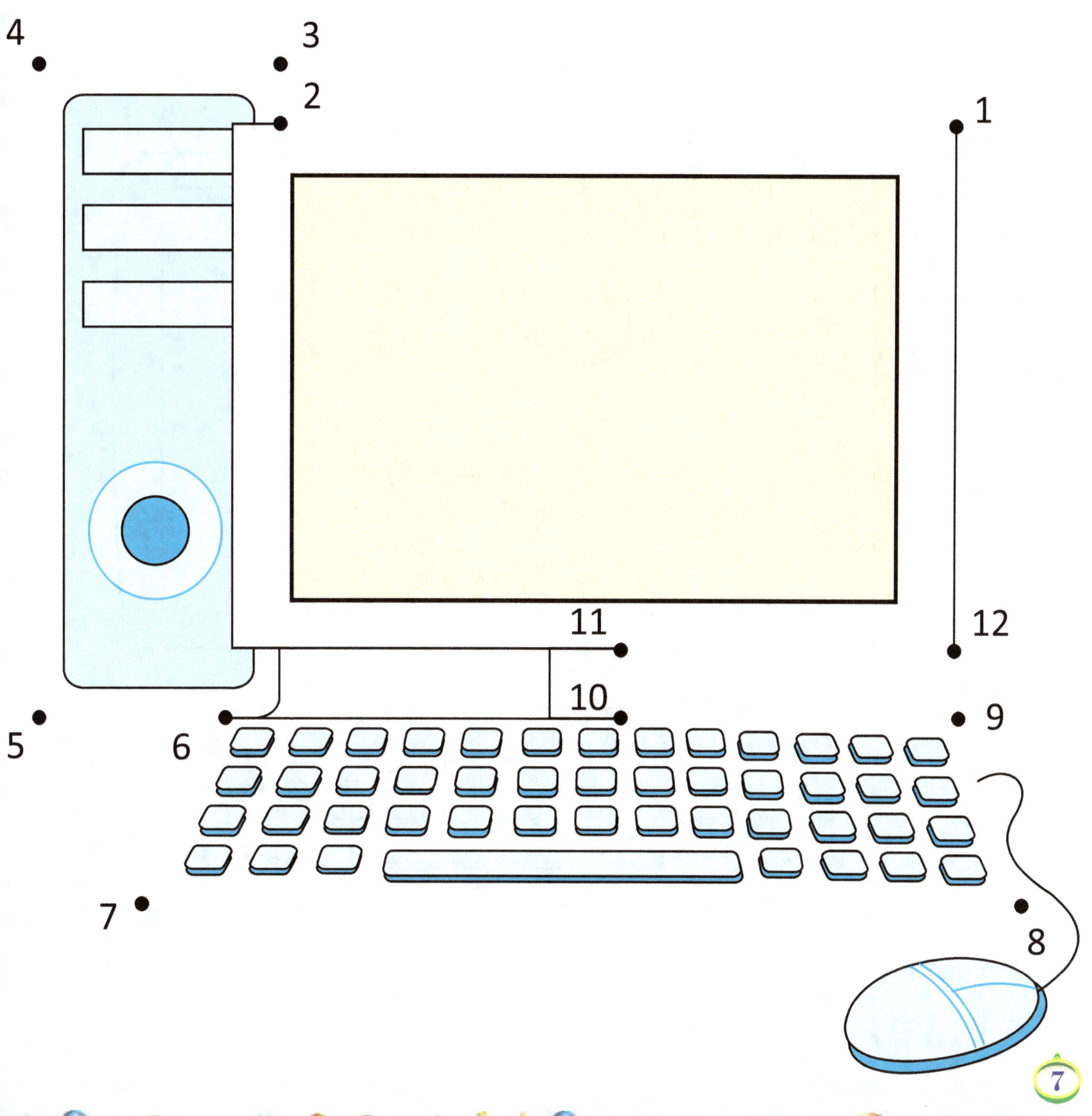

This is my picture.
Please make it colourful.
Hi !

Colour the letter C.

Trace the letters of Computer.

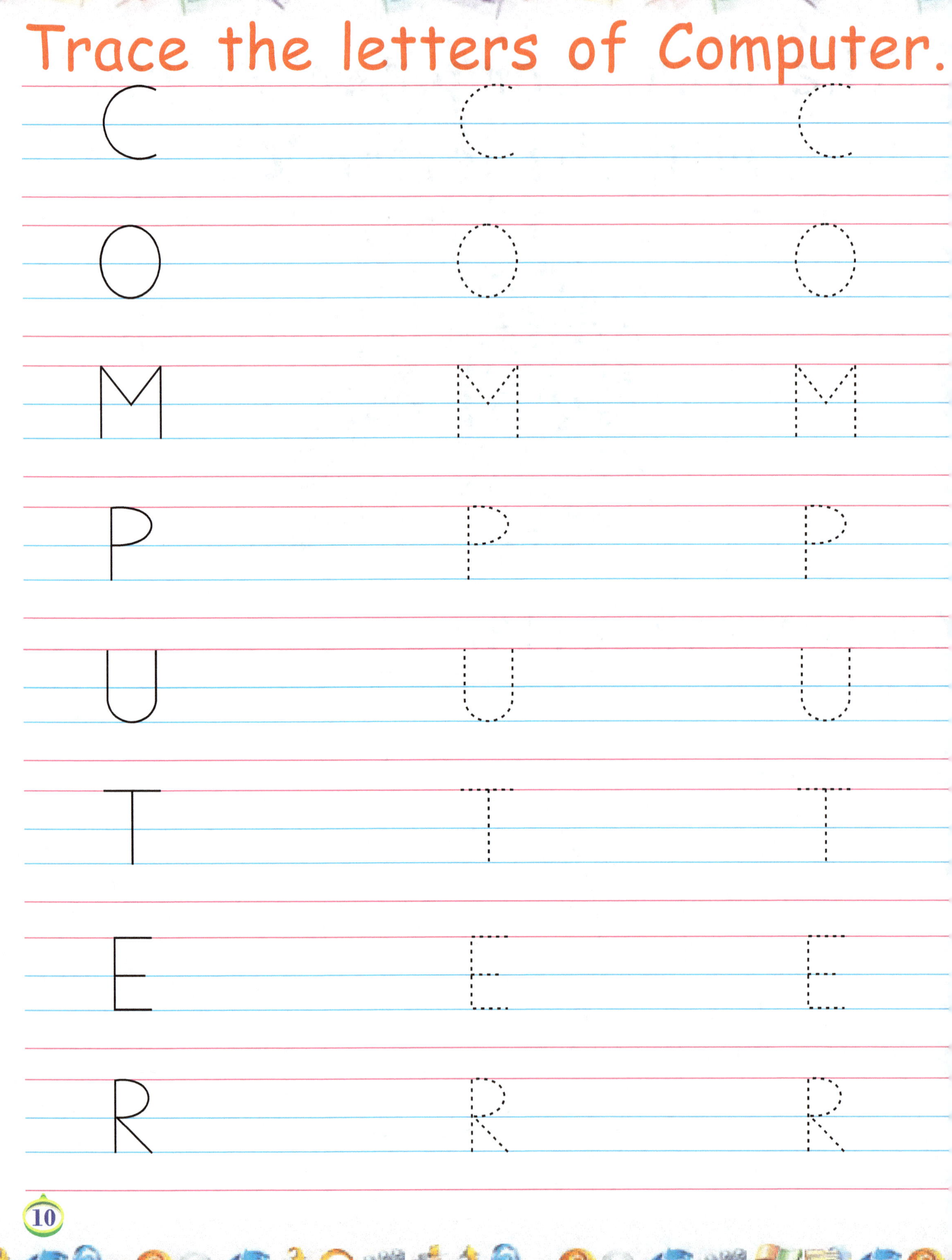

THE MACHINE

The Computer is an **electronic** machine.

It makes our work easier and faster.

Car

Bicycle

Motor bike

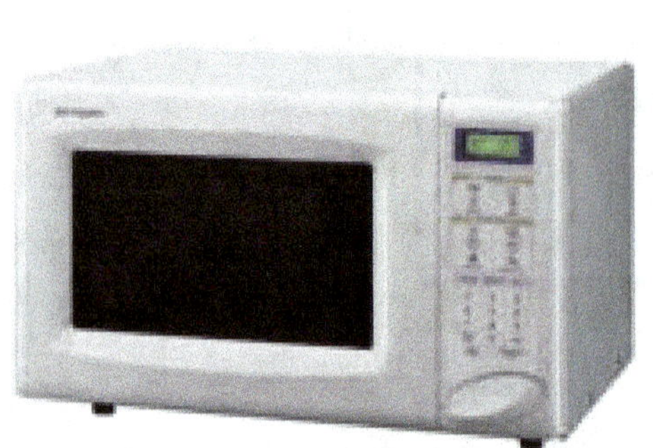

Microwave oven

Vacuum cleaner

Mobile phone

LED (Television)

Music system

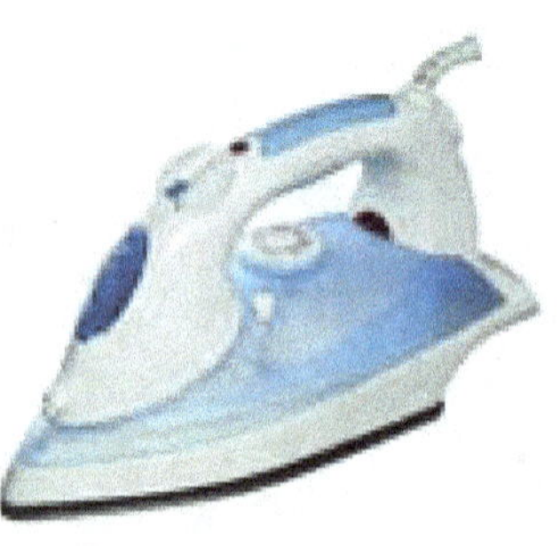

Steam Iron

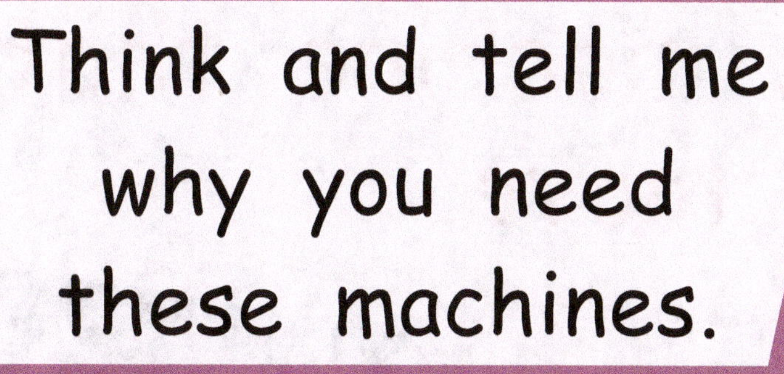

Think and tell me
why you need
these machines.

These machines
help us to finish our work
easily and quickly.

Tick [✓] the machine that helps you to **move**.

Tick [✓] the machine that helps you to **talk**.

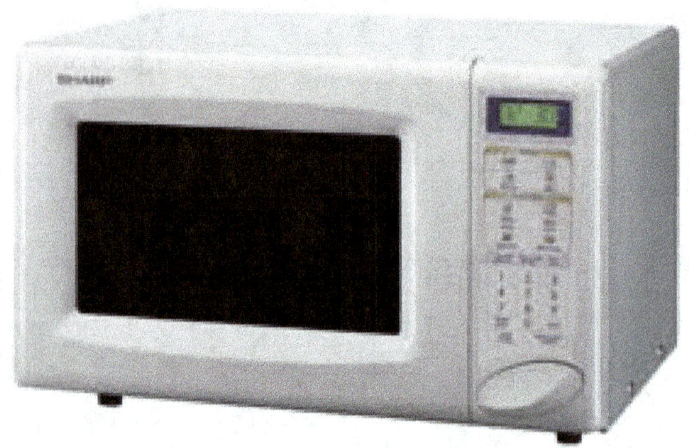 

Colour the machines.

Now, trace the letter M.

Colour the letter M.

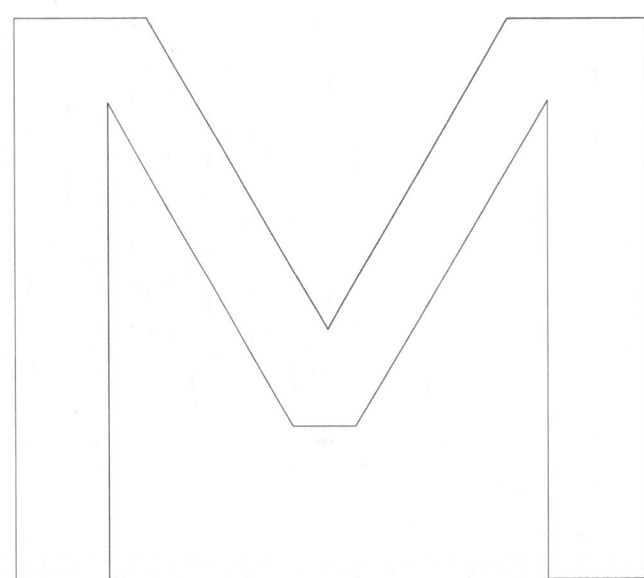

Trace the letters of Machine.

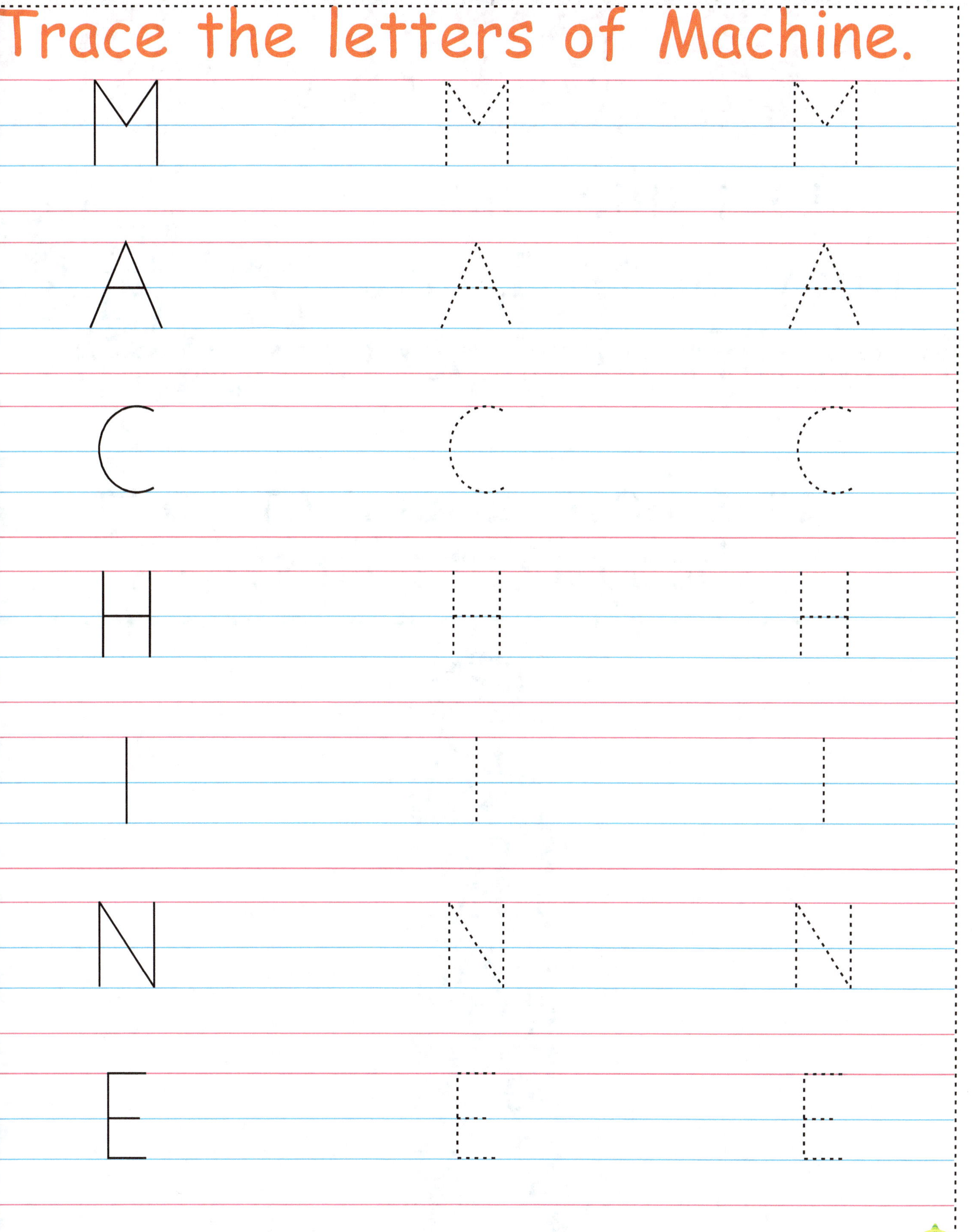

MEET MY PARTS

Just like your body-parts, I also have different parts.

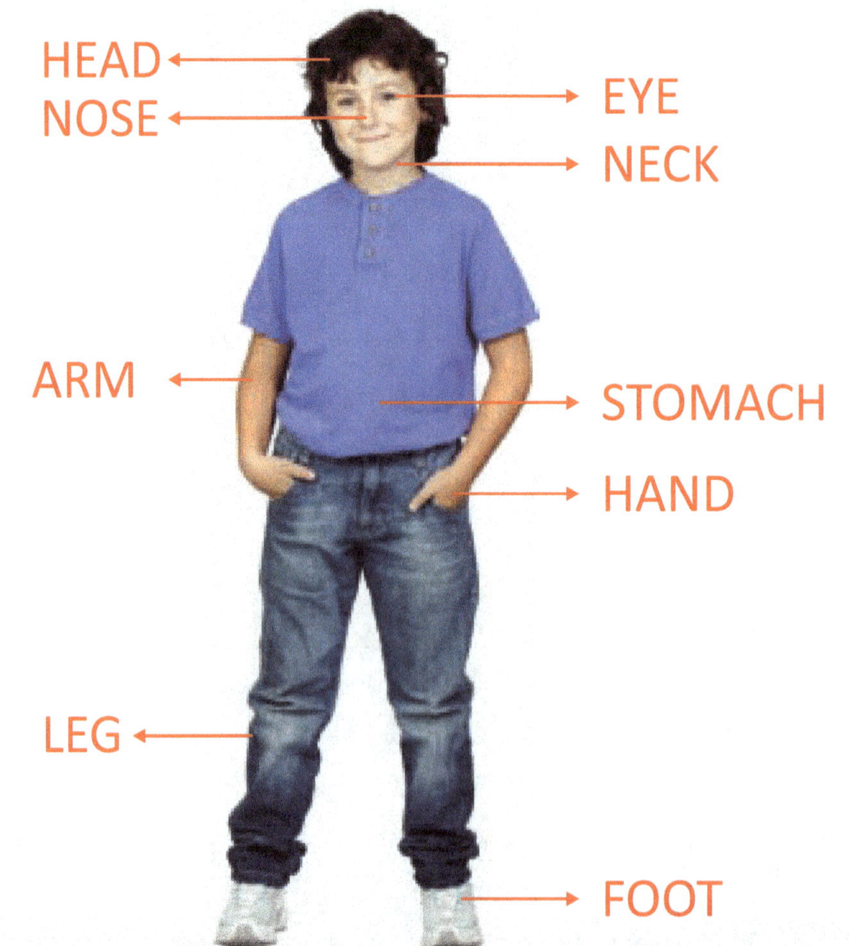

Let's have a look at your body-parts first.

Now, I shall tell you about my parts.

This is a **Monitor**.

You can watch cartoons and read stories on the monitor.

> # A monitor looks like an LED (Television).

Monitor

LED (Television)

Join the dots and colour the picture.

Colour the picture.

The word 'Monitor' also starts with the letter 'M'.

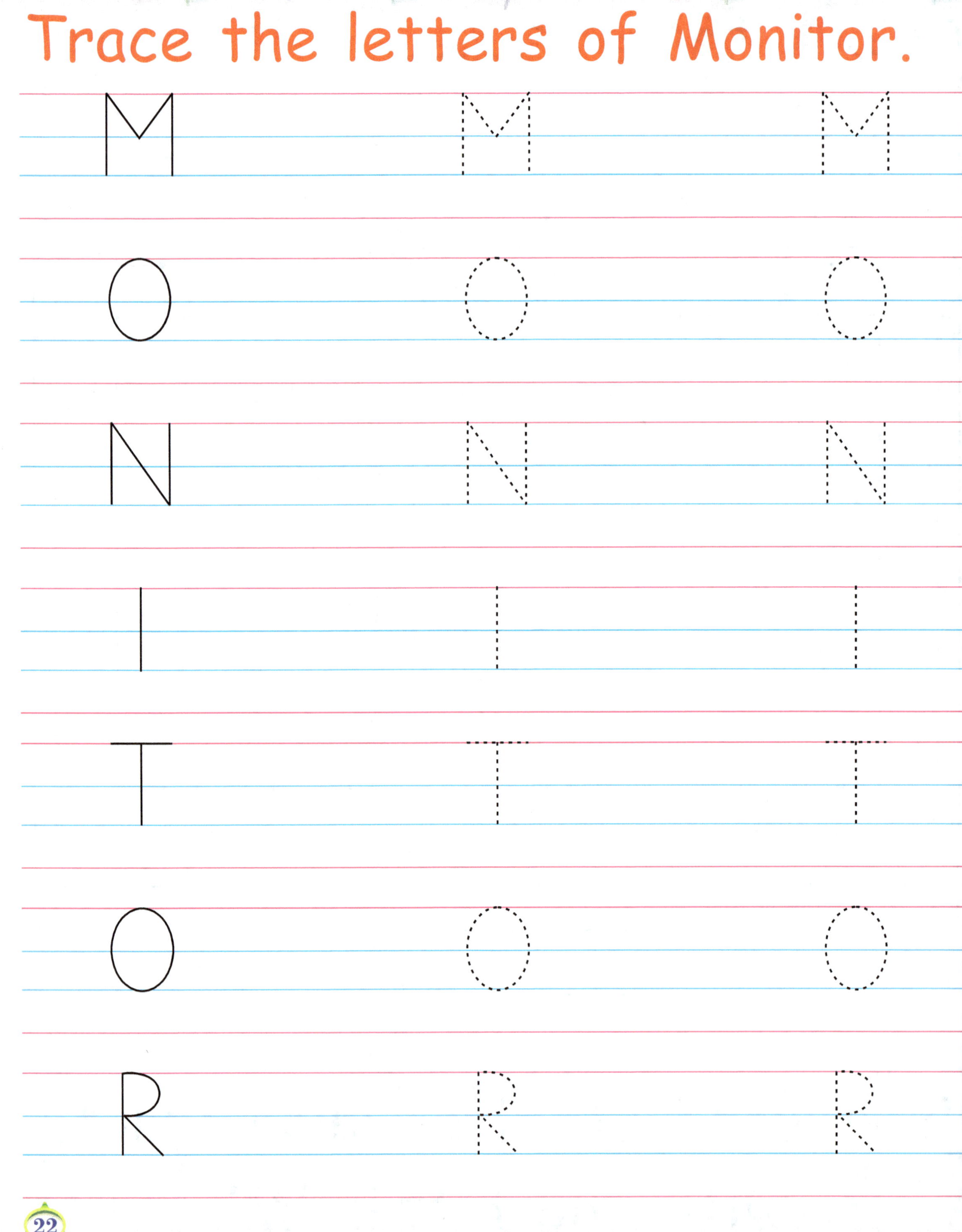

M   M   M
O   O   O
N   N   N
I   I   I
T   T   T
O   O   O
R   R   R

This is a Mouse.
You move it to work in the computer.

The mouse has a small body and a long wire.

Oops ! Don't compare it to the mouse in your house, that eats your food and spoils things.

Join the dots and colour the pictures.

The word '**Mouse**' starts with the letter '**M**'.

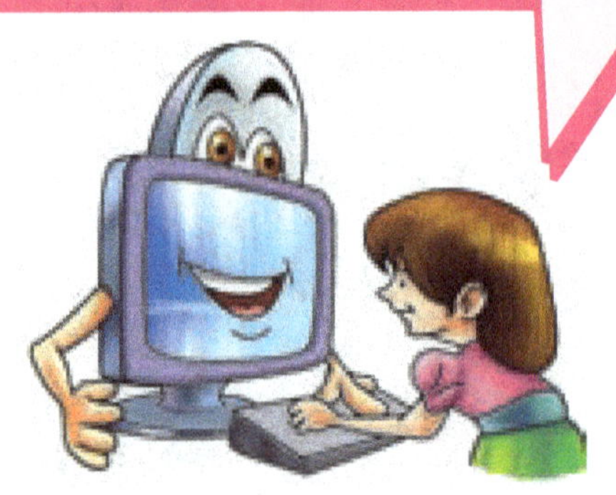

Trace the letters of Mouse.

M M M

O O O

U U U

S S S

E E E

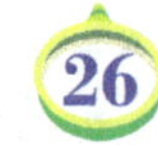

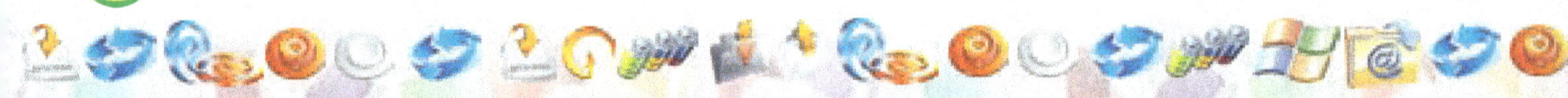

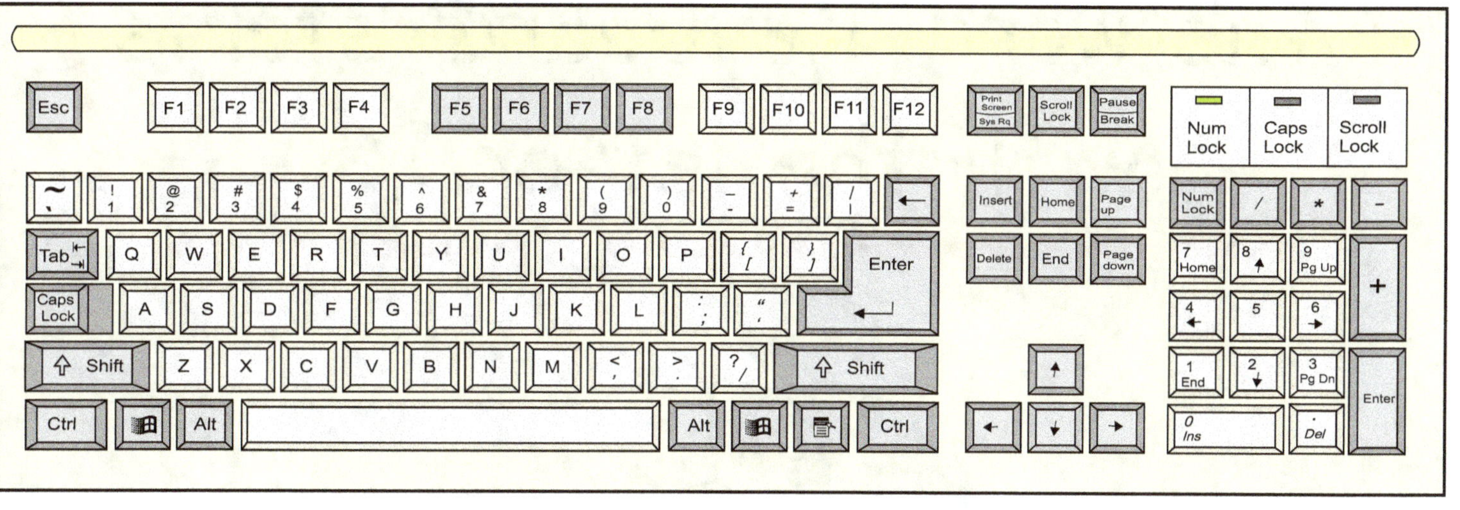

This is a Keyboard.

You can use it to type words and numbers into the computer.

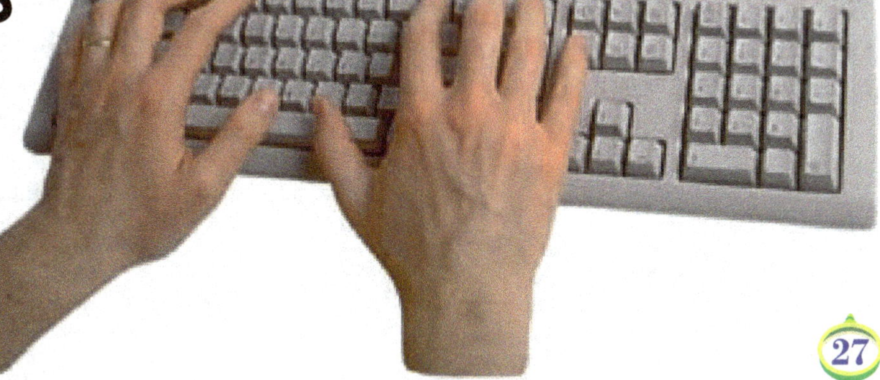

Colour the Keyboard.

Now, trace the letter K.

Trace the letters of Keyboard.

K   K   K

E   E   E

Y   Y   Y

B   B   B

O   O   O

A   A   A

R   R   R

D   D   D

This is a CPU.

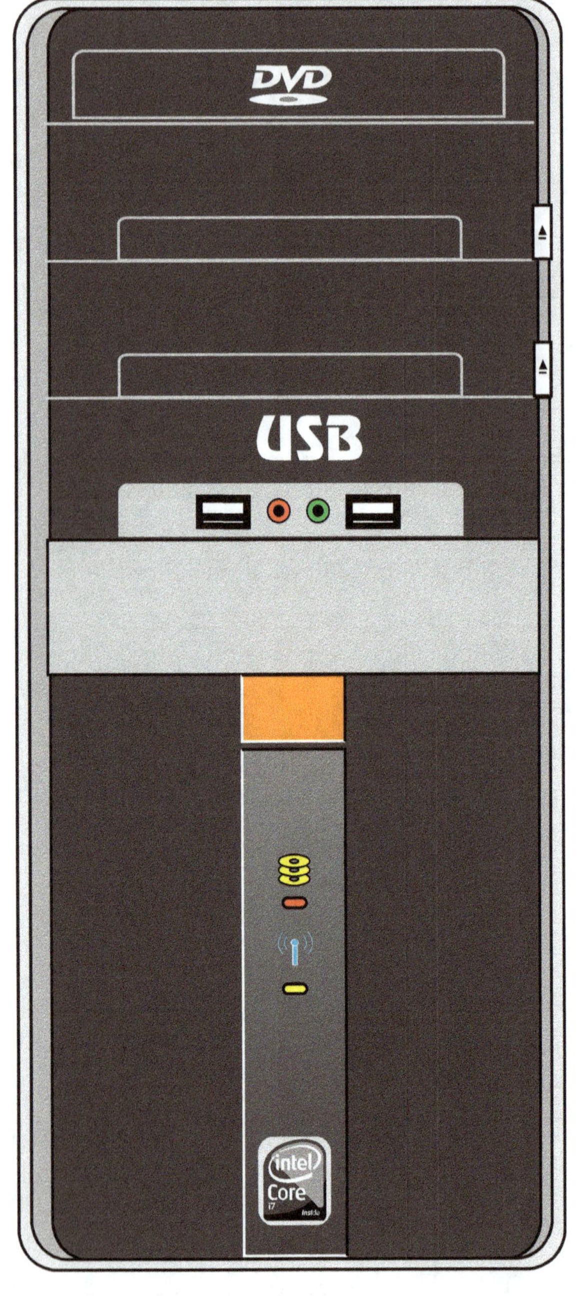

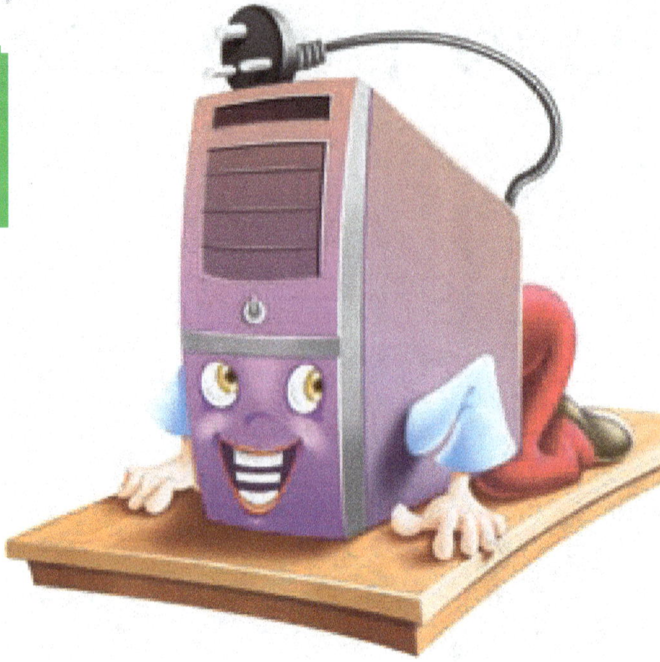

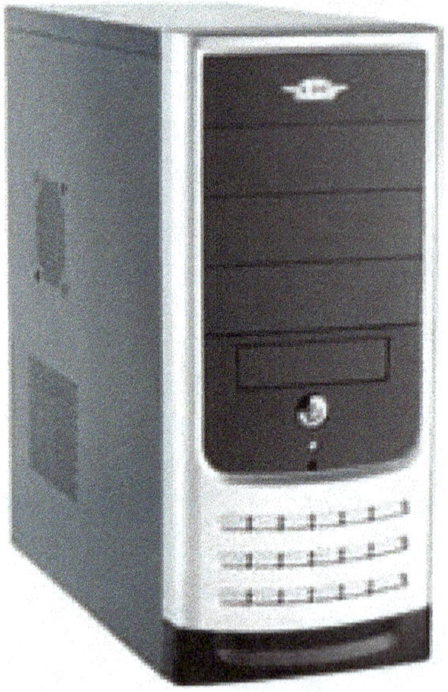

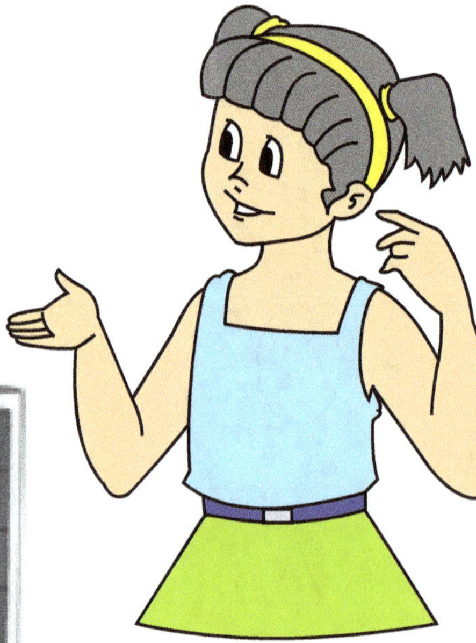

What is a CPU ?

CPU stands for Central Processing Unit.

I do all my work with the help of a CPU.

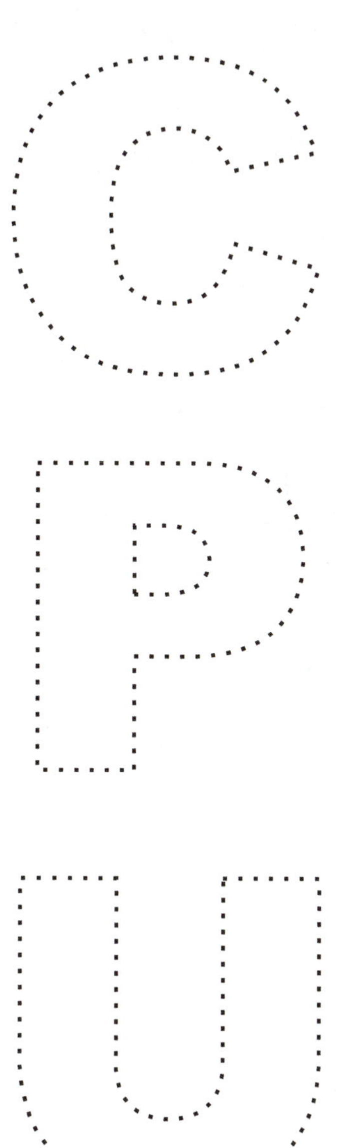

Join the dots and colour
the picture as well as the letters.

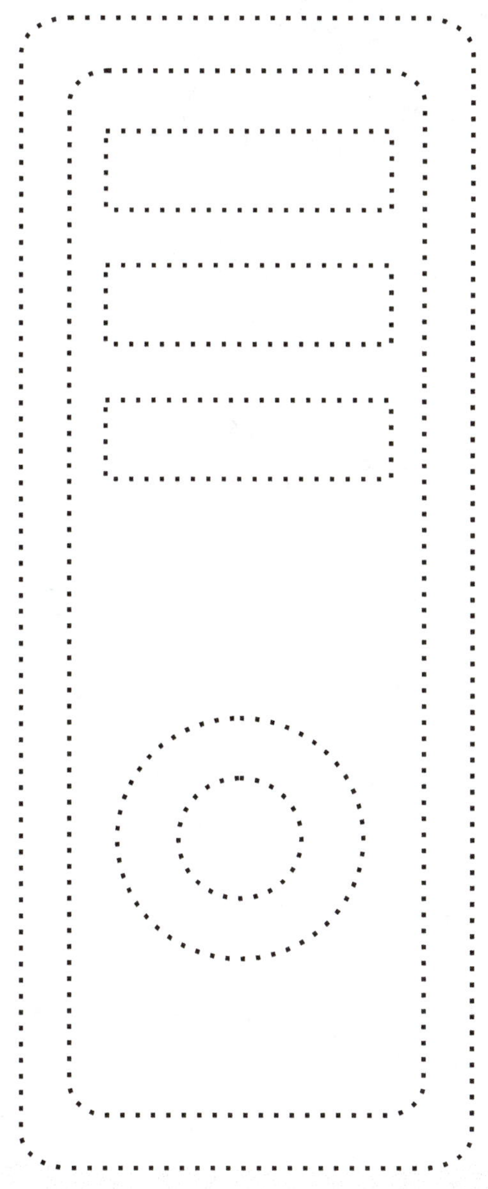

Now, trace the letter C.

Trace the letters of CPU.

C

P

U

Kids, I have so many computer parts with me. Can you help me to find out their exact number?

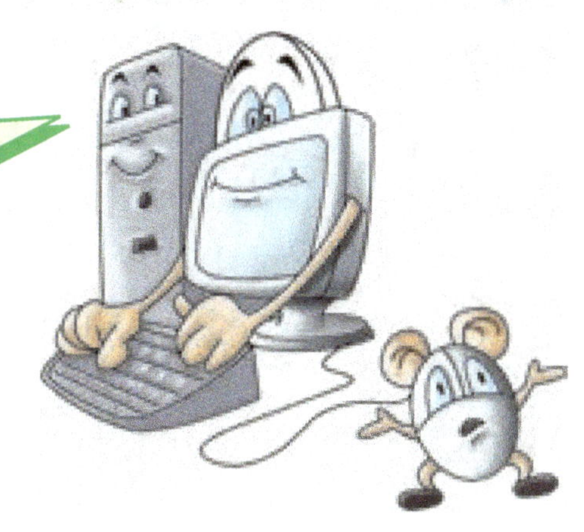

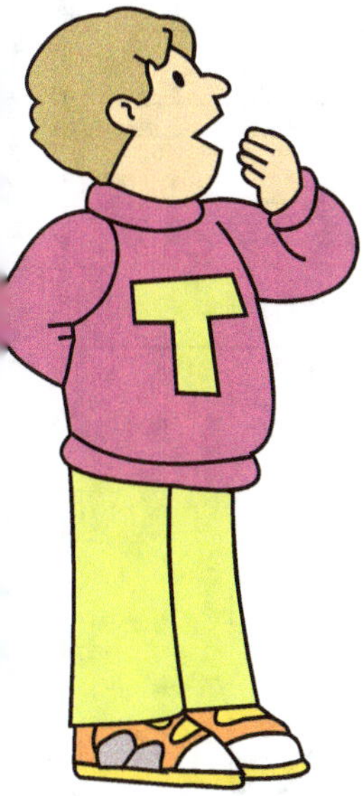

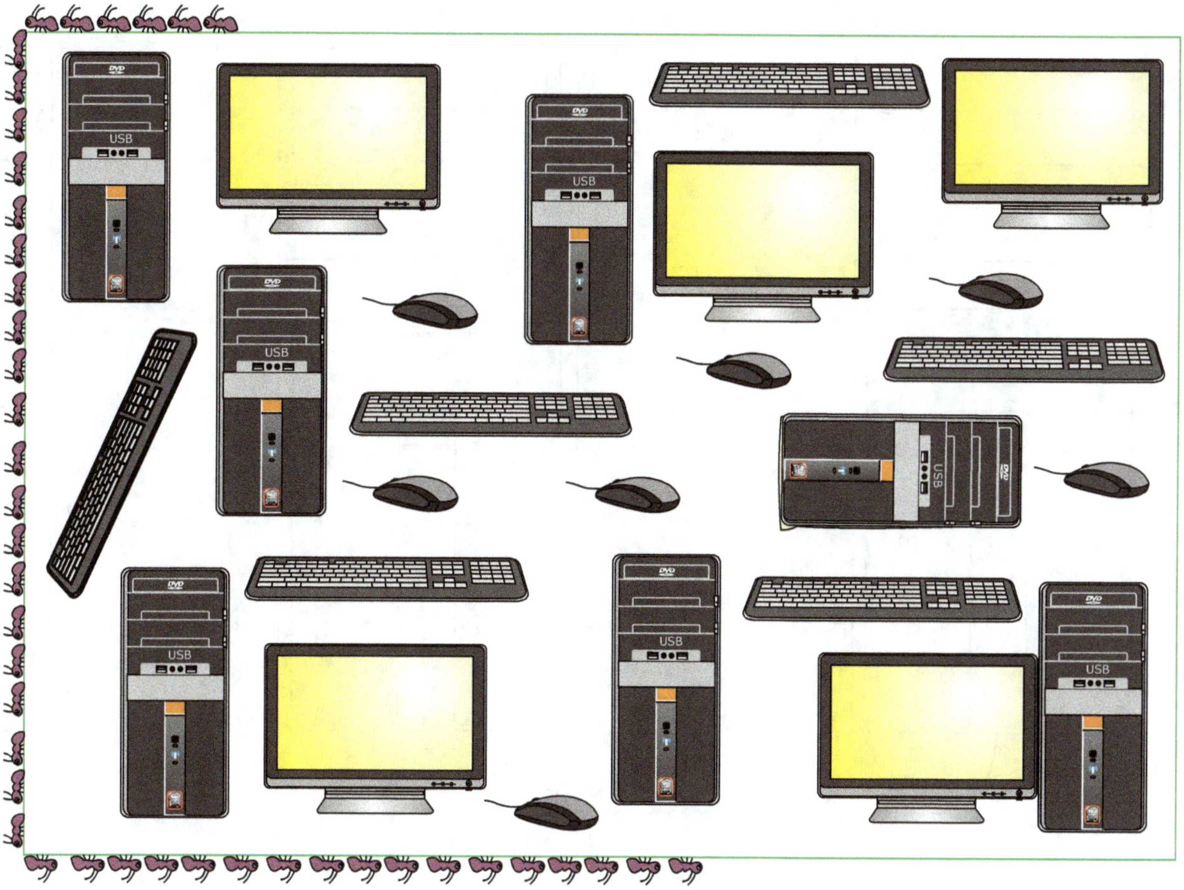

Number of Monitors ....

Number of Keyboards ....

Number of CPUs ....

Number of Mouses ....

Find the mouse of each CPU and colour the CPU with its respective mouse the same.

Match the computer parts with their names by linking the shapes.

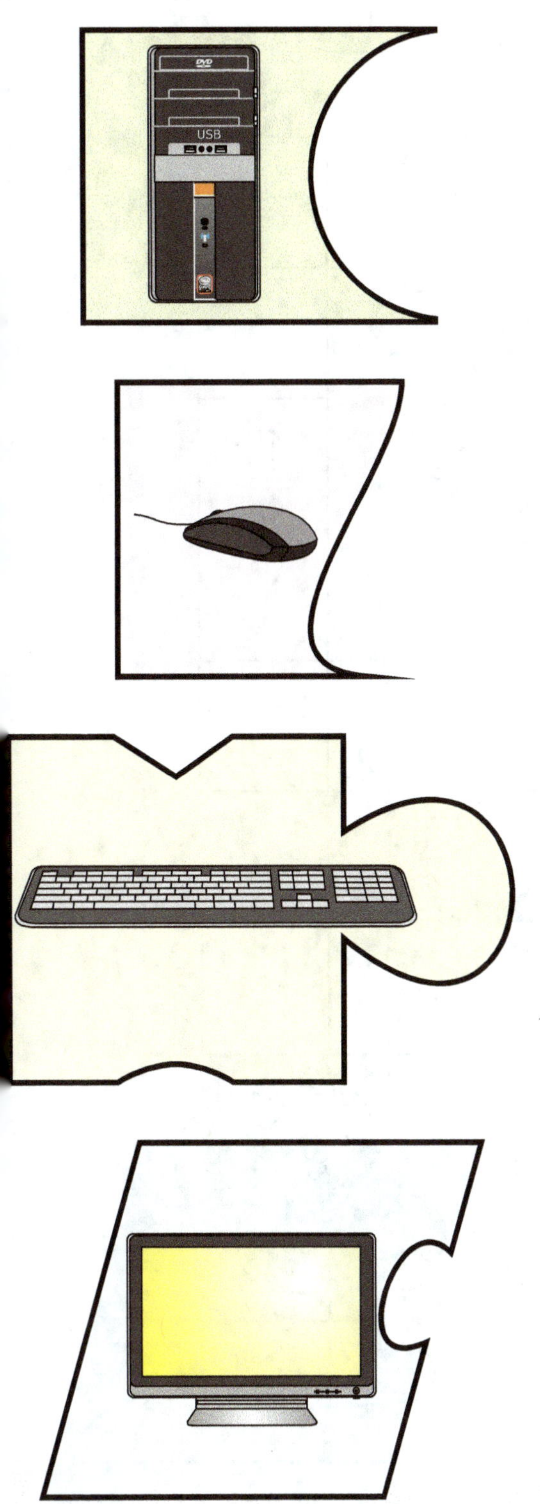

Follow the path around the animals that like water. Trace the letters.

K E Y B O A R D

C
P
U

M O U S E

M O N I T O R

1. You can write words and numbers.

2. You can play games.

3. You can listen to songs.

4. **You can watch cartoons.**

5. **You can draw and colour pictures.**

Help the boy and the girl find me.